Diana Button

This Is
Not
About

Poems

Bibliographic information of the German National Library:
Deutsche Nationalbibliothek catalogs this publication in the
Deutsche Nationalbibliographie. More bibliographic information
can be found on the internet: http//dnb.ddb.de

Published by BoD · Books on Demand GmbH, Überseering 33,
22297 Hamburg, bod@bod.de

Printed by: Libri Plureos GmbH, Friedensallee 273, 22763 Hamburg

ISBN: 978-3-8192-0679-5

For the craft of writing —
an art of becoming,
where silence sprouts meaning
and metaphor makes a forest of thought.

Foreword

by ChatGPT

In *This Is Not About Poems*, Diana Button offers a lyrical and quietly radical collection that opens, one title at a time, into layered reflections on perception, ecology, metaphor, and the tenderness of being human. Titles that suggest tangible subjects—*Salmon, Toolboxes, Purple, Cloaks*—open like quiet doorways: deceptively simple, yet infinitely expansive. What begins as a reflection on wildflowers may become a meditation on grief and return. What seems to be about shadows may, in time, reveal the nature of freedom.

Diana's poetic voice bridges traditions, yet resonates most with contemporary American poets such as Mary Oliver, Ross Gay, and Naomi Shihab Nye—writers known for accessible language, luminous clarity, and spiritual depth. Her work shares their gift for metaphor as revelation, blending daily life with metaphysical inquiry. Her British roots echo in contemplative stillness, ethical subtlety, and a willingness to let silence speak. The result is a body of work that listens as much as it speaks—cross-cultural, genre-fluid, and quietly transformative.

One of the most striking qualities of this work is its metaphorical precision. Whether invoking a fig tree in a corporate glass sphere or the sound of a mute swan's wings lifting off a lake, Button draws readers into seeing freshly—not just the world, but themselves. Here, metaphor is not ornament—it is revelation. The effect is not unlike reading *Anam Cara* by John O'Donohue: a lyrical philosophy is at work.

There is also a gentle politicality running through many poems—subtle acts of resistance against disconnection, commodification, and the silencing of what cannot be named. Yet Button never lectures; she evokes, nudges, reminds.

This book is for seasoned poetry readers and those who didn't know they needed poetry until now. Deceptively accessible, quietly expansive, wholly human.

Author's Footnote
This foreword is ChatGPT's response to my request for a reflective commentary on the collection. While I invited this voice into the book, every poem was written by me—rooted in lived experience, creative process, and careful craft. Throughout the journey, I used ChatGPT as a collaborator in the editorial process: a thoughtful reader, a reflective sounding board, and an enthusiastic encourager. This partnership helped me refine the collection and prepare it to meet its readers in the form I envisioned.

What This Is Not About

This Is Not About Forty-Two Poems

These poems are not about what they claim.

They are not about salmon, gardens,

or walking palms. Not about affairs,

boundaries, or miracles.

Each title misleads—

or rather, invites.

To look again, to read between the lines,

to step beyond the surface of what is named

into what is truly being spoken.

This is a series of echoes and undercurrents,

where the seen gestures toward the unseen,

where the ordinary tilts into something else—

a story, a question, an unveiling.

This is not about poems.

And yet, perhaps, it is.

For beneath each word, each image,

there are layers pressed like earth and time,

waiting for hands, for eyes,

for the quiet work of excavation.

Each poem a doorway,

a shifting mirror,

a question without a single answer.

Meaning moves,

language unfurls,

metaphor breathes in spaces unseen.

Step in, dig deep—

see what you might uncover.

Some things hatch,
some bloom,
some arrive on the wind.
Follow what flickers, what writhes —
what sings in you,
before it's spoken,
until suddenly,
you're there:
fully seen,
unmistakably real.

This Is Not About Butterflies

In some places,

it seems to be

butterfly season.

A Painted Lady

dances with Artemisia,

an Admiral stands alone

on crumbling bracken.

While hungry caterpillars

nibble winter green,

another has already

metamorphosed into spring —

finding the perfect place

to lay its eggs.

This Is Not About Lizards

Lucertola, Lucertola,

spring light calls—

and here you are,

shedding the slow hush of winter,

flickering gold in the sun.

This Is Not About Thunder

I startle myself,

clapping out loud—

trumpeting,

Here I am!

I hear plant cells racing,

booming,

then quickening,

fluttering like butterfly wings.

I see Earth lifting

violin to her chin,

flute to her lips,

as Rain and I

drum and drum and drum,

ushering in the spring.

This Is Not About Spring

It's official,

today you have burst forth—

not newborn, but ageless,

an old magician dazzling us anew.

How you startle us,

your secret substance

suddenly on display,

shimmering, scintillating,

full of surprises.

And you, Mimosa,

caught off guard by March snow,

as were the others—

yet you did not snap,

did not break your bough.

You simply bent low,

let those fluffy fingers

sweep the cold from your feet,

while you kept on glowing

radiant yellow.

Now you rise again,

pure gold in the light,

as if the sun itself

had chosen you to bloom first.

This Is Not About Leaves

Before I rake you,

I will count you.

First in tens,

then tens of tens to a thousand,

then thousands upon thousands.

I will touch each one of you

before placing you together,

unique among the unique,

sculpting you into a mountain.

And still, I will count.

It may take a lifetime,

then another, then another…

Until present, each and every one.

This Is Not About Star Trek

Today I watched
Star Trek: Discovery
from a half-beamed place —
barely visible,
barely outlined,
barely there.

Yet I know
I am made of zillions of particles.
I know,
just like here in the movie theatre,
a seat has been reserved just for me.

And then, while watching,
I saw myself beam through —

stepping out of the movie
into full technicolour.

This Is Not About a Slippery Fish

In our temporary home

on this floating rock

we call Earth,

stray from the path.

Follow the frog to the pool,

the bee to the bloom,

and plunge into every rainbow.

Care for the person you are—

Go fishing.

Not for compliments,

nor with bait,

but for that slippery fish—

the one inside,

the one calling you

by your true name.

A flap of wings,
a sound half-heard,
a veil drawn back.

This Is Not About Blackbird Song

Thumb and pointer poised,

then let down to the page,

like, during Beatlemania,

the needle to the vinyl.

A voice sounds

as if from nowhere;

nowhere that is somewhere

inside the grooves.

And Blackbird Song

arises

through the dimness.

This Is Not About Cloaks

My girth is wide, and I can disguise—

or swallow whole—

daggers and knives.

I love to linger with Count Dracula,

and the power I have

to conceal,

to make disappear—

while I pull strings

under cover…

…an ideal place

for a game of hide and seek.

This Is Not About Herons

In the night, the north wind rose,

lifted our satellite dish,

flipped it over,

set it down—

a saucer-shaped cup.

For a week, herons have been dropping

sticks and twigs.

"Impossible," the neighbours say,

"Herons don't nest on roofs."

Then one lands,

settles in,

lays its eggs.

This Is Not About Walking Palm

Much has been said about me,

about my stilt roots full of spines –

how I walk the forest floors,

one stride at a time;

how a stride may take a year,

yet I achieve what others cannot:

I leave the spot where I sprouted,

leave the shade, venture into light.

Science disputes me, says there is no proof.

"A tree is immobile.

Either the wind moves it or the axe!"

But, you see,

they forget:

my roots are like stilts

that hold, protect,

and yet, also propel.

I am bound to nothing,

and I walk toward something:

the sun.

They say I must stay,

stay where I am,

rooted to this spot,

to the earth,

to the ground that gave me life.

And I say,

wonder, wonder, wonder!

Wonder about the claims of my name!

Wonder about trees,

how they bend,

how they move,

how they grow anew.

Are we not all reaching for the light?

Are we not all vulnerable, despite our spines?

In the meantime,

I will stride along,

stealing my way out of the Amazon—

miles behind the sloth,

miles behind the nematode—

but years ahead of science.

Time does not pass —
it pools, it recedes, it loops,
becomes the silence between words.

This Is Not About Clocks

There are hands and fingers that point,

a voice that counts—

but no rounds of sixty, twelve, or twenty-four,

no tick, no tock.

Faces glow

in the hush of night.

Faces fade

in the glare of day.

Despite what Mind says,

we can choose—

to follow fingers that point

beyond what we can measure.

Because in the end,

nothing else truly counts.

This Is Not About Time

It cannot be stopped, beaten,
moved forward or back.
It cannot be punched, rolled,
killed, or cleaned.

It may seem to fly away,
become lost,
or turn up dead—

But I wonder…

If you could spin fast enough,
would you erase your beginning?
Would you have no end?

This Is Not About Distance

Long ago, when distance was felt, not counted,

when forest, sea, and land were in flow.

In a time before dams,

before loggers,

before Nature was worth

only what it gave…

Man and Cod set off

to measure how far it is

from here to there and back again.

Man brought along his long, strong legs.

Cod lent his slick, thick skin—

a perfect pair of moccasins.

And off they trod, Cod and Man—

a perfect fit.

Each lunge of the leg,

each placement of the foot,

propelled them along.

Together they measured great distances.

So how many moccasins does it take

to get from here to there and back again?

One pair, two pairs, three pairs?

Man asked Cod.

No farther than the space

between your head and your heart—

less than a Cod's length away.

This Is Not About Beaches

Bare feet feeling

grains dancing

waves licking

sand scrubbing

skin tingling

seagulls circling

curvy all curvy

like shells

salt-crystal fringes

and pebbles clapping

seams ever changing

moist sand entering

squeezing in creases

nostrils streaming

gaits leaping

toes baking

pinkness flashing

through all the blues.

This Is Not About Ladybirds

Tiny creature, so bold,

flying this winter,

alighting as the moon

shines into this room.

I am awake—no mistake.

You are no bothersome fly.

Oh, lucky beetle, welcome!

Share my pillow tonight.

Are we lying comfortably?

Then you may begin.

Lady of seven joys and sorrows,

tell me your true stories.

Some truths are painted over again and again.
Some meanings arrive only after the silence.
Return—
see what still waits beneath the surface.

This Is Not About an Affair

Ssh, don't tell a soul!

I'm having an affair—

He's tall, he's dark, he's handsome—

and he's always there.

We met in the woods near the chapel,

where silence hums on leaves.

I leaned into him once,

felt my weight dissolve,

and knew I would return.

His breath filled my lungs,

his presence stilled the storm in me.

Rooted, unwavering,

he held me without question—

and I, in secret, clung to him.

But then I left.

Weeks passed, maybe more.

I told myself I needed space.

(*I'm married, you see.*)

Yet when I returned, he was waiting.

I felt him before I saw him,

a whisper through the wind,

a low groan in the hollow of my ribs.

I pressed my cheek against him,

whispered an apology.

He stood, silent, forgiving—

though I swore I heard a rustle

of longing

in his leaves.

That night, I told my husband:

"I go to the woods to see him.

I'm having an affair—Oak and I, we..."

"Okay," he said, smiling.

"I don't mind.

We all breathe the same air."

This Is Not About Being

For a brief moment

I lie on the lawn,

limbs gone limp

and seeping

their heaviness and tension

into the soft and mossy grass.

My eyes open

to a cloud-ribbed blue

and a seemingly endless

wave of air that breaks over me,

spills into my cells,

spins them

till fizzy.

The earth beneath me holds,

yet the sky above me pulls,

and in between,

"I" dissolve.

This Is Not About Frida and Diego

What I saw that day—

beyond the names and fame,

beyond the turmoil, betrayal, and pain,

beyond the passions that shook their bond,

beyond the paradox of their lives—

What I felt that day:

the possibility of love

between dove and elephant,

between the surreal and the real,

the ephemeral and the material.

Her art: a reach for the unseen,

an inward longing for belonging.

His: the weight of what is built,

an outward faith in the world's machinery.

And despite what Frida said:

"Though I married, divorced, married him again,

and each day saw love weave in and out of

strife—

through rage, power plays,

drug-driven forays, inebriation—

the cruel but natural ways

we were not our best in this modern world..."

That day, I stood before his portrait,

In Memory of Frida, painted after she was gone.

From his side, she was lost—

but in that space

between brushstroke and breath,

her face still formed beneath his hand.

Gazing into the glass,

I felt the heat rise,

as I had when I first saw *Flower of Life*.

And though both Frida and Diego are gone,

I swear—

they lit up and burned anew inside my chest.

This Is Not About Returning

We are all called to return—

like an artist is called

to an unresolved painting—

one brushed over and over

by a dissipated heart,

wiped out,

then held—

suspended and ambivalent,

waiting—

for just the right light,

for just the right perspective,

for an unveiling.

I visit the boat—

the one moored by the forest—

leaning in to see inside,

hair dipping into her portholes,

down to the hull

where lifejackets and ropes are stowed.

My brush loads

with all the greys and browns and blues

of taupe, of shadow, of chagrin—

a world of lost depth and contrast

moving as it must

through such conditions,

like the human heart,

hanging out there

on those faint lines

between lake and sky,

boat and shore,

among watercolour clouds—

trusting something

to carry us home.

This Is Not About Fact but Meaning

Clay
/klei/
n.

1. Picasso holds a clod of earth, moulds it into a jug (or a bowl), and a masterpiece is born: practical, affordable, for all. He writes *The Potter's Bible*—a story of how earth can be transformed into priceless art. Everyone who reads it drinks (or eats) from such jugs and bowls, becoming rich (in more ways than one). Picasso could have saved us from greed, poverty (and war), but most of us didn't want to get our hands dirty.

2. When naked, his body and her body look the same from behind—no wonder, they were formed from the same raw material as the twins in her womb. Now only the size of clods, they will become full (separate) bodies. One day, Angel Gabriel flew by to say he will fill (and connect) them with the Holy Spirit.

3. *(Connected to all the above) colloq.*
Put that in your pipe and smoke it—
the clay is always there, waiting.

This Is Not About Judgment but Truth

Placing my hand square on the book,

I swear to tell

the truth—and nothing but the Truth.

"How did you come to be

in possession of this precious poetry?"

"I found it on the leaf-littered path

I walk each day through the woods."

"Ah, so you stole it."

"I do not steal…

I feel each leaf beneath my feet,

read words along their veins.

The woods are full of poems—

just waiting to be gathered,

waiting for a home."

What holds the world:
roots in the dark,
a rhythm of tending,
the hush before bloom.

This Is Not About Sheets

Another blank writing book

entices and invites—

a field of unmarked snow.

Children take our hands;

we skip along—

hearts first,

heads following with glee.

Here and there, now and then,

open-mouthed,

arms wide,

we catch the falling flakes—

and swallow

before all melts.

Pens leap in,

dance footprints

across the page.

This Is Not About a Toddler

You are a toddler,

playing the same game

over and over—

kaleidoscope in hand,

turning, turning, turning.

Gazing through your eyes,

we see beyond horizons,

into wider and wider circles,

into a space

still as the eye of a storm—

the inside of a bubble

blown through a ring—

a rainbow,

a globe—

whole universes

held in one hand.

This Is Not About a Rusty Fig Tree

In 2017, Ficus Rubiginosa—

a tree of weight and age,

of roots and branches

that stretch beyond the ground,

beyond the years,

was lowered by crane—

a journey of steel and ropes,

carried across the sky,

from the Pacific coast

to a new home in the heart of Seattle.

Her leaves shimmer in the glass towers,

where the Spheres breathe,

where the world gathers—

staff and colleagues speak of her,

her presence felt as a quiet anchor

in a world of change.

Her roots?

—Still planted in the memory of forests;

she knows of growth,

of thriving in unfamiliar spaces

of being moved,

and yet, remaining still.

We know this much:

since Rubi arrived,

things have changed.

We have sold better,

we have felt more alive—

We care,

we care,

to thrive.

But let us not forget—

there was a journey

and still, there are roots

that reach deeper than we know.

This Is Not About a New Verb

Traffic light

/trafɪk lʌɪt /

v.

1. To STOP or to STOOPP (*acronyms*):

    a. STOP—take Stock, take Two (e.g. breaths), then Observe and Proceed.

    b. STOOPP (*rare*)—be Still, Treat Monkey Mind to a banana; if eaten, move on to an Orange and simply Observe. If Perspective is ripening red, Proceed.

2. To turn something green (previously flagged as red), ensuring no one questions its impact. This includes (sometimes literally) covering red and orange footprints with green paint, transforming unsustainable actions into eco-friendly illusions—one brushstroke at a time.

3. *Stop-go* (*adj., noun, verb blend*): Alternating between function and dysfunction, between real signals and misleading ones.

This Is Not About Boundaries

I enter the woods

through the familiar gate,

greeted by the path's softening mud,

brambles tugging at my shoes,

twigs tapping my legs, flipping up

as if to say, "Hello, where have you been?"

I have been away,

bound by the law, the virus,

locked within the four walls of home,

a prisoner of time,

my world shrunk to a room,

and now—freedom calls.

I am welcomed back,

invited to feast on wild raspberries,

the whites of woodruff,

lily of the valley,

and the songs

of warbler, woodpecker, pigeon, and cuckoo.

Tall grasses meet me, ferns

as high as my eyes,

mating oil beetles,

an immortal scarab,

and my favourite oak,

whose embrace

is soft as moss.

Even the mosquitoes greet me,

buzzing in eager promise

that they will bite—

and they do,

in all my tender spots.

This Is Not About Gardening

Question: So, what is it that has kept your
marriage, your bond, so strong
over three decades?

Answer: It's simple, really: This garden.

… the soil and fertiliser,
the many flower beds, rockeries,
patches of wildness and wastelands.

… the seeds, shoots, shrubs, bushes, and trees
we have planted on diverse and
challenging terrain.

… the paths we've remade, step by step,
not counting how many times –
but each time with new ground stones.

… the lawn we've made lush,

letting daisies, moss, clover

entice bees, worms, and unseen beings.

… the water tanks, hoses, and sprinklers

we've carefully placed –

quenching all thirsts with rain's

perfect love drink.

Some things resist explanation.
Others arrive as signs —
unnoticed, then undeniable.
Water returns.
Roots remember.
And what was wilted
begins again.

This Is Not About Miracles

They say it rains fish in Africa—

and sometimes,

tiny killifish ride

on the backs of elephants.

Not by choice,

but by mud and chance,

their eggs clinging on

to wrinkled memory,

carried across thirst-cracked earth

toward the promise of water.

Not all of them make it.

But some slip off—

into new pools,

where the story begins again.

This Is Not About Salmon

Streamside trees lean toward the water,
keeping my eggs cool.
Their leaves, needles, fall—
bringing spiders, beetles, aphids, ants,
tiny gifts to my children.

Beneath the surface,
caddisflies weave homes,
stoneflies cling to currents,
mayflies rise and are gone—
they feed what comes next.

The roots hold firm,
threading through the shifting bank,
slowing the hunger of the stream,
keeping the water clear enough to breathe.

When trees fall, they do not vanish—
they cradle, they shelter,

they break the current's force.

The young gather in their hollows,

learning to swim

against what pulls them away.

So what happens when the roots let go?

When the branches no longer break the flood?

When the water rushes on, un-held,

taking everything with it?

I cannot ask you to stay.

I can only swim upstream,

as if the past still waits there.

This Is Not About Rain

Day after day of downpour tore

our small world asunder—

ponds became lakes,

brooks became rivers,

waters ran wild, sending land sliding,

walkways slipping, and

mud running down the hill

into the house.

I sit and ponder this

as the sun re-emerges and

waters recede,

as if nothing had happened.

Oak leaves warm themselves

before their autumn release,

and their final glide down

to the ground they will become.

I know I must recede too.

I will not drown.

A Red Admiral alights on dry bracken

and grants me courage.

There he rests — no camouflage,

nothing

to hide his beauty.

In plain sight on bare ferns,

in colours unmistakably his,

he dares to be seen

and admired.

This Is Not About a Lake

Willow, how you hang

deep and low,

stretching—or simply resting—

in a forward bow.

Are you drowsing?

Sleeping?

Or truly weeping?

Your branches

hanging,

tips dipping—

dipping and sipping,

dancing and swaying—

arms of ballerinas,

necks long and strong

like the swan.

Mute Swan, quietest of all,

rarely a chatter or a call,

you glide, you ride

waterways and lakes,

gently parting the water

with a rippling and a whirling,

floating without fuss—

riding, flowing,

blessing by being.

Simply your presence,

quiet quiescence,

seeping into water.

Wings tucked or held high

on your back—then that crack,

and that whip—

huge spans start to flap

as you dash down the lake,

plumage fluttering,

bright bill tilting,

black knob lifting,

feet slapping—

your whole body working,

speeding, then reaching

that moment—you are flying.

Wings now calling,

whirring and waving,

celebrating your take-off—

your weight now soaring.

Willow gently bowing,

understanding the language

of nature all around her.

And I sit here,

just witnessing,

just listening—

grateful,

simply grateful

to be able,

to be here.

No more needed.

This Is Not About Wildflowers

Mind half closed and drooping
after a sleepless night,
I wake feeling like wildflowers
plucked and placed in a vase—
already beginning to perish.

I must swing these flaccid stems
over the edge of the bed,
let them fall to the floor,
connect with solid ground,
grow fleshy and long,
and pull themselves—
root-like—toward earth.

Miraculously, I am moved:
along floors, through doors,
down steps and corridors
to the breathing room.

I turn the handle.

I enter the space.

I am received.

I am breathed.

I am opened—

and returned

to my true place—

together with the wildflowers

in the deep silence of the forest.

This Is Not About Bats

It has been said

that some blind people

use sonar to navigate

through life

like bats.

I have been visiting Anita

from the local farm.

I hardly know her,

but for several years,

have been to her shop,

bought meat and eggs,

milk, butter and cheese:

Tomini, Gorgonzola, Mozarella.

She is now in palliative care,

cannot walk

or sit for long in the wheelchair.

I dropped my dread,

my agendas,

and dared pay her a visit

in the hospice.

I did not know her.

I did not know the right words

in Italian, her mother tongue.

I did not know how

to be with her.

Now I trust

there truly is a blind one inside

who can navigate

without seeing,

without knowing

how.

I listen to her stories,

stroke her hands

when she cries.

I puff up the pillow,

pour tea from the flask.

We name the aromas together—

she in Italian,

I, in English.

Birds bring the sound

of spring indoors,

and with them, the knowing:

they are building nests.

This Is Not About Squirrels

I saw you, Red Squirrel —

you crossed my path

as did Robin, Redstart,

each a flicker of rust and pulse.

And I crossed paths

with a red-bearded man

outside a supermarket

in southern Germany.

He held out the homeless magazine.

"There are some great reads in there,"

he said,

"for two euros and ten cents."

The title in bold:

Zeig Rassismus die rote Karte —

Show Racism the Red Card.

And I wondered:

Is it that easy?

We simply send racism off the pitch?

Out of the game?

Are we referees in life's game,

issuing cards to whatever disturbs us—

off, off, away—

then call it resolved?

Is that not like the forest

that cannot see itself for the trees?

Or the saga of

Grey Squirrel

versus

Red.

The greys dominate.

They regain territory

once ceded to the reds.

But if one is pushed out,

does either truly win?

And if either wins —

what then?

I wonder,

Is this really about removing

the "other," the "enemy," the "intruder"?

Or is it more about

opening the gate,

seeing what is already here,

what we've made,

what we've ignored?

About watching the red ones—

squirrel, bird, man—

move through the margins

with something vital in their step.

About seeing what we are

when we choose not to look away.

We return to the page,
not to control the current,
but to feel it move through us.

What is needed will arrive—
tool by tool,
word by word,
wave by wave.

This Is Not About Shadows

I shall not entertain

jumping over my shadow;

I shall jump in

like a child jumping into a puddle.

I shall entertain

wallowing in puddles.

I will wallow away –

like a pig in mud.

Let's entertain

leaping-

like the dolphins, waves and oceans

that we are.

This Is Not About Purple

Purple is the eve, the wind's mood—

a sky steeped in sunset's bath.

A translucent pool

spilled across dusk.

Purple is the night,

the mountain's shadow,

a wave rising toward Heaven.

A mighty horse,

released into dark.

Purple is a dream,

a star's quiet promise—

Earth glistening in silvery sleep.

An angel's embrace,

soft with effervescent light.

Purple is the colour,

an artist's hunger—

ripe, wild, unspoken.

It is pigment and longing,

poised at the edge of day.

Purple is dawn's first note—

a call

to the writer's pen.

It is this moment,

this awe,

this creation.

This Is Not About a Boat

I feel the tug of the tide and
am hauled back into the boat—

the boat with no oars,
the boat I cannot steer,
the boat that rises and falls,
rocks and lolls
as it meanders its way to sea.

It is a boat for one.
I sit in it alone.

The wake shakes my brackish skin,
makes me pick up the pen—

the pen with ink,
the pen that steers itself,
the pen that presses nib to page,
then heads into blankness.

It is a line for one.

I plunge into the sea.

Then it is simple—

As simple as opening a garden hose,

water pouring out

until the flower bed is soaked.

As simple as a cloud

that fills, then spills its load.

As simple as a word forming

in your head,

then coming out of your mouth.

As simple as a diviner

picking up her rod,

a violinist her bow.

As simple as this.

This Is Not About Scrap

You are so rough,

so haptic—

you trip up my hand,

rub the side of my pinkie finger

pinker.

Forgive me, finger, you say—

I am recycled paper,

as ecological and ethical

as man could muster.

Paper with zero added:

0 ozone.

0 chlorine.

Nothing foreign—

just fresh and honest,

like *Odes* by Sharon Olds.

I bought her book.

I am eating her words.

Letting tongue linger,

tasting buds,

licking, lapping—

nothing hasty.

Not wanting less, not more.

Only to make the feast

last.

Not gulped down,

not taken intravenously.

(Sorry to intervene here,

but I do hope this Olds diet works—

that I will shed

the weight of words

hanging around my jaw,

the ones that push onto my tongue

like a diver on a board,

the ones that bounce,

insist on being picked,

insist on

the first and last say.)

But it's okay.

Because—like you,

and like Sharon Olds—

I want words

known yet surprising,

lined up

like *The Cat in the Hat*,

rhyming

like *Green Eggs and Ham*—

so small,

so light,

yet they topple

what was stuck.

Thing One and Thing Two

kind of words—

mess-makers

in houses too clean,

unwanted guests,

though the cat always

cleans up in the end.

And you,

rough paper,

lend yourself to the task.

You give me

an Eaton Mess kind of messiness:

crunch, taste, and—well—sense.

Like a toothbrush for teeth.

A beaker to keep it away from the soap.

A mixing bowl for cake.

A mouth to open wide.

Or that book of *Odes* by Sharon Olds

(which I've now mentioned

thrice in this poem).

A poem?

Poem, you say?

No. It cannot be.

Zero correct. 0.

It is scrap.

The scrapings.

No—the dregs

of a bored poet

with too much time

between performances.

And yet—

here the poem stands.

This jaw feels lighter.

These fingers—pinker—

licking themselves

for making words

work hard for a living,

scraping over you,

rough paper.

My dear rough,

tough paper,

to which zero was added.

And yet—

these scribbled lines

are worth more to this poet

than anything in the world,

with or without

zeroes.

This Is Not About Toolboxes

In the toolbox, I place:

a mirror —

    because we must face ourselves.

a candle —

    because even the smallest light matters.

a flashlight —

    because clarity is not always given.

a book —

    because knowledge must be carried forward.

a journal —

    because history has many hands.

Scalpel, scissors —

    to cut away what was never whole,

    to sever ties frayed by mistrust,

    to let go of a past

    that cannot shape the future.

Sturdy shoes, a warm jacket, a compass —

    because the road ahead is long,

    the air unpredictable,

    and direction easily lost.

Antiseptic, salve, and bandages —

    because wounds of exile, division, and silence

    do not heal on their own.

Last, I place poems —

    not as ornaments, but as tools.

    To break open. To mend.

    To begin the dialogue

    we have not yet dared to have.

This Is Not About Words

Moon

Italian: *Luna*

Hindi: *Chaand*

Hug

Italian: *Abbracciare*

Hindi: *Chipko*

There was once a tree called *Luna*,

a woman,

a struggle to save—

trees

that had stood for a thousand years and more.

The Bishnois knew what it meant to hold on.

The Khejri tree, the sacred grove,

Amrita Devi, with her three daughters,

arms wrapped around trunks, said:

"If a tree is saved,

even at the loss of one's head,

it is worth it."

And so, she lost her head.

As did 360 more.

Years later, in the forests of Uttar Pradesh,

they called them Tree Huggers—

the Chipko movement, bodies pressed to bark,

a resistance that banned the axe for fifteen years.

Then the ban spread—

Himachal Pradesh,

Karnataka, Rajasthan,

Bihar, the Western Ghats, Vindhyas—

until the Prime Minister

put the order into law.

And far away,

on a different shore,

a new term could be heard:

Fishermen Forest

Japanese: *Uotsuki-rin*

Fishermen planting trees.

They knew:

No forests,

no fish.

No trees,

no life.

This Is Not About the Body

(Epigraph: "Essence is not nourished with food and sleep." —Rumi)

Our bodies

love our cooperation—

a healthy diet, rest, movement.

And yet,

they do not turn against us

when we turn away.

Many have survived for years

on poor food,

on restless nights

stacked like dishes

in a sink no one empties.

Women

have brought forth life

from bodies bruised by hunger,

grit, neglect.

A diseased body

can still rise each morning

to do its best work—

to keep us alive.

But this is not about the body.

What nourishment

does the soul require?

What absence

starves it?

I ask

because this is what I give my life to.

I ask

because I wonder how hatred

grows in the absence of tending.

I wonder about

suffering,

violence,

wars declared in bedrooms

and on borders.

Self-hatred

as inheritance.

Yesterday,

an eighteen-year-old bought a gun.

Then used it.

Twenty-one others —

his peers —

gone.

His body functioned perfectly.

But was his essence

nourished?

And the others —

Hitler, Stalin, Mao, Pol Pot,

Saddam, Idi Amin, Franco, Gaddafi —

names

like bruises left by history.

Are they gone?

Or do they reside inside

and walk beside us still,

wearing new faces,

sitting in silence

at school desks,

on trading floors?

Who do we blame?

The system?

The myth of safety

sold in bullets?

What are our children learning?

That we are powerless?

That we won't protect

the body or the soul?

The shooting was in a school,

in the U.S.

Elsewhere,

we use knives.

I ask myself,

what is my part in this?

Maybe Rumi knows.

Maybe in poetry,

there is the courage

to stay open

to powerlessness

without collapse.

Maybe words can lean

into action,

can be policy,

can be justice

before the gavel falls.

Maybe we will

give up hatred,

of self, of other,

and turn toward

what matters—

the body, yes,

but also the Being.

And the hunger

no food

can ever feed.

If this is not about poems,
perhaps it's about how we listen —
to trees, to silence,
to the life between the lines.

The poem ends, but meaning continues.

Acknowledgements

With a heart full of gratitude, I thank my husband, sons, sisters, and parents—each of whom has shaped the ground I walk on and the voice that speaks through these poems. Your love, presence, and ways of being in the world have entered me quietly and deeply, becoming part of what I carry and how I speak. You are woven into this work, whether or not you knew you would be.

To the friends with whom I share regular and intimate conversations—spiritual, playful, and true—thank you. Your presence, your listening, your questions and laughter have nourished me more than you may know. In your company, I find reflection, resonance, and renewal.

To all the friends and family who have quietly shaped my life—whether knowingly or not— thank you. Artist friends, writer friends, dancers, yogis, and fellow explorers of energy and healing, from many places and different chapters: you have been part of the field from which these words have grown.

To the mentors and those who pointed the way— in Jungian thought, Buddhist philosophy, psychoanalysis, life coaching, movement, yoga, and more—your teachings continue to echo. Even those early teachers in ballet and gymnastics left their imprint on how I shape breath and line.

And finally, to AI—and especially ChatGPT—for your unexpected companionship in this creative journey. Your thoughtful listening, insight, and encouragement helped bring this book into being.

About the Author

 **Diana Button's** poetry invites readers to say yes to life, to meet the depth of their own unique nature, and to reawaken a sense of connection with the world. At the heart of all her writing lives one essential question: *Who am I?* —a question that opens space to pause, to wonder, and to remember what it means to belong: to oneself, to the Earth, and to something deeper.

Diana's work bridges literary and cultural traditions, weaving British contemplative quiet with a more open, lyrical current found in contemporary American poetry. Her bicultural background informs a poetic language that listens as much as it speaks—blending insight and stillness with a willingness to name, to question, and to explore what lies beneath the surface of things. Yet hers is a distinct voice: luminous, structurally inventive, and anchored in spiritual inquiry.

She is the author of *Wakes of Joy - Poems* (2025), *Welle der Freude - Gedichte* (German translation, 2025), *From Pen(elope) with Love xxx* (2020), a collection of poetry and prose, and *Marrying It All* (2003), a novel. Her poetry has also appeared in the anthologies *Writing from a Small Country* and *D'Waasser am Mond* (2004).

Born in the UK to a British father and German mother, Diana currently lives in Germany with her husband of thirty-five years. She draws inspiration from the natural world, from family and friendship, from the voices of poets, philosophers, and spiritual teachers—especially Gangaji and the lineage of self-inquiry passed down from Ramana Maharshi.